Lonicera

CLIMBING HONEYSUCKLES

Denis Bradshaw

NCCPG National Collection Holder

Photographs by Denis Bradshaw
Drawings by Rosemary Lindsay

CONTENTS

Introduction and habitat 3

Cultivation and planting 3

Planting uses 4

Pests and diseases 5

Pruning and feeding 5

Classification 6

- Group 1a Flowers in pairs, unscented. Evergreen 8
- Group 1b Flowers in pairs, fragrant. Evergreen 9
- Group 2a Terminal heads or spike, unscented 11
- Group 2b Terminal heads or spike, fragrant 16

Some honeysuckles for different positions 23

Some honeysuckles in combination with other plants 23

Bibliography 23

Index 24

Lonicera - Climbing Honeysuckles

Honeysuckles have been grown in our gardens for many centuries because of their powerful fragrance and ease of cultivation. The word itself evokes thoughts of summer evenings in cottage gardens and country hedgerows, the air filled with their rich perfume.

However one of the earliest introductions, *Lonicera sempervirens*, is not fragrant. This was grown by John Tradescant in the late 16th century and was valued for its bright orange red flowers.

The word 'honeysuckle' is probably derived from the Anglo-Saxon word 'hunigsuge', whilst the country name 'woodbine' perhaps came from the Scottish word 'widbin'. In contrast the French name 'chevre feuille' means goat-leaved as does the family name Caprifoliaceae, to which honeysuckles belong. The genus is *Lonicera* and was named by Linnaeus after the 16th century German naturalist Adam Lonizer.

Habitat

Many species climb by twining their stems round branches of woodland trees reaching up into the sunlight. Some will grow into dense thickets and layer themselves along the ground, others in more open positions will scramble into hedges or sprawl over rocky outcrops. The berries produced by many provide an excellent source of food for both birds and mammals. The flowers, particularly fragrant from dusk onwards, attract a wide range of insects, especially hawk moths which are the main pollinators. These in turn are a good food source for bats. Some of the brightly coloured North American honeysuckles, e.g. *L. sempervirens* and *L. arizonica*, are not fragrant and in their natural habitat are pollinated by humming birds. In Britain the bees puncture the sides of the long tubes to get at the nectar and in doing so fail to pollinate the flowers.

Cultivation

Most honeysuckles are hardy and will thrive on soils rich in humus, with moisture available in the growing season. Whilst the native species, *L. periclymenum*, grows happily on clay, the southern European forms, e.g. *L. etrusca, L. implexa*, need more sunshine and will tolerate drier conditions. Some species, particularly *L. tragophylla*, need shade to grow well in the south, but if there is sufficient moisture during the summer they will grow in more open or sunny positions.

Because honeysuckles are shallow rooted, a cool root run is preferable and it is important not to plant them too deeply (unlike clematis). Strong climbing forms, e.g.

View of the nursery stockfield.

L. japonica, L. × *italica, L. periclymenum* 'Graham Thomas', should not be planted with weak growing or very choice plants. Other forms, like *L.* × *heckrottii* or *L. sempervirens*, would be more suitable.

Planting

All honeysuckles are pot-grown and may be planted at any time of the year, providing they are well watered. Autumn planting is ideal for drier counties, spring for very cold or wetter areas. Immerse the plant in a bucket of water and prepare a hole two or three times the pot size and slightly deeper, making sure the hole is 50 cm away from wall foundations. Incorporate some organic matter, e.g. compost or rotted manure, in the bottom of the hole. Remove the pot carefully; if the roots are tightly matted loosen the bottom ones and then place the plant in the hole, making sure it is just below soil level (i.e. 2-3 cm). Backfill with a mixture of soil and organic matter, treading firmly in. Then water very thoroughly. If planting in summer be prepared to water several times until the plant becomes established and starts to grow away. Start training young shoots into their desired position. Most plants will benefit from a general all round feed during the growing season (see page 6).

Planting uses

Pergolas, archways, walls and fences are natural choices. Dead tree stumps, rough boundary hedges can also be used to great effect. Poles or tripods set in borders can give good vertical emphasis and *L. periclymenum* 'Belgica' has been grown in standard form at Het Loo in Holland and also at Hampton Court. *Lonicera sempervirens* f. *sulphurea* is grown with great effect through a yew at the Hillier Arboretum, the dark foliage offsetting the yellow flowers. *Lonicera periclymenum* 'Serotina', and *L. implexa* would be very suitable for tub planting on patios and both are fragrant. Although *L. japonica* and its forms are very rampant (a weed in some parts of the USA) they are some of the most useful for screening trellis or hiding oil tanks. *Lonicera japonica* 'Acumen' and 'Dart's World' can be very useful when grown as ground cover.

Pests and diseases

Thankfully most honeysuckles, given good conditions, will grow quickly and easily with very few problems. However **aphids** can be a problem. The North American orange-red forms seem to be the most susceptible, e.g. L. *sempervirens, L. × brownii* 'Dropmore Scarlet' and *L. ciliosa*. If these are planted in half shade and sufficient moisture to encourage vigorous growth, this will help minimize the problem. Other forms like *L. × italica, L. etrusca* and *L. japonica* rarely seem to suffer, so in dry positions it is better to plant these. Occasionally thrips, leafminer or capsid can do a little damage but not generally enough to worry about. A proprietary insecticide spray applied in April/May should overcome most problems with aphids or other insects.

Powdery mildew may sometimes be a problem, particularly when the plant is under stress from dry conditions. *Lonicera ciliosa, L. splendida* and *L. japonica* 'Aureoreticulata' are the worst affected forms. Again half shade and plenty of moisture and perhaps a precautionary spray with a mildew fungicide towards the end of June or early July will reduce the problem. Alternatively plant less susceptible forms (see p. 23)

Several fungi can be the cause of **black leaf spotting**, but they tend to be specific to *Lonicera: L. caprifolium* and its forms are most affected. Remove the old flowering growth in April/May, which will encourage new strong healthy growth. Spray with a rose blackspot spray at this time and again just before leaf fall in the autumn, this last spray will help to reduce overwintering spores. The alternative is to plant other varieties.

Pruning

Is it necessary and why? In time most honeysuckles develop old and hollow woody stems. The flower quality diminishes and the plant loses vigour. It is then more prone to disease.

The very vigorous forms of *japonica* can be cut back annually with shears. This can be done after flowering in October/November, or if in a very cold position can be done just before growth starts in the spring.

Most other forms will benefit from cutting back old flowering growth either

Honeysuckle (left) before pruning and (right) after pruning.

immediately after flowering or in the autumn when the birds have finished the berries. During the winter, very thin twiggy growth and any diseased stems can be cut out and any over vigorous growth can be shortened by one third. *Lonicera sempervirens* tends to keep on flowering, very often through the winter. I find it is better to cut back some of this flowering growth in early spring. This reduces the older overwintered shoots and encourages healthy new growth for flowering from May onwards.

Feeding

Early spring is a good time to start feeding honeysuckles. Blood, fish and bone or a complete balanced proprietary fertilizer is suitable. Be careful not to put it too close to the main stem where it may scorch the fine surface roots. Water in well if the ground is dry. A further top dressing of fertilizer may also be beneficial around June/July, but do water it in well and make sure the plant is not under stress.

Classification

The genus *Lonicera* contains about 180 woody species of which 50 or so are climbers, the rest being of shrubby habit. They grow throughout the temperate regions of the northern hemisphere, crossing the equator only in the Malayan Archipelago, where it reaches Java as its most southern point and northwards extending to the Arctic circle.

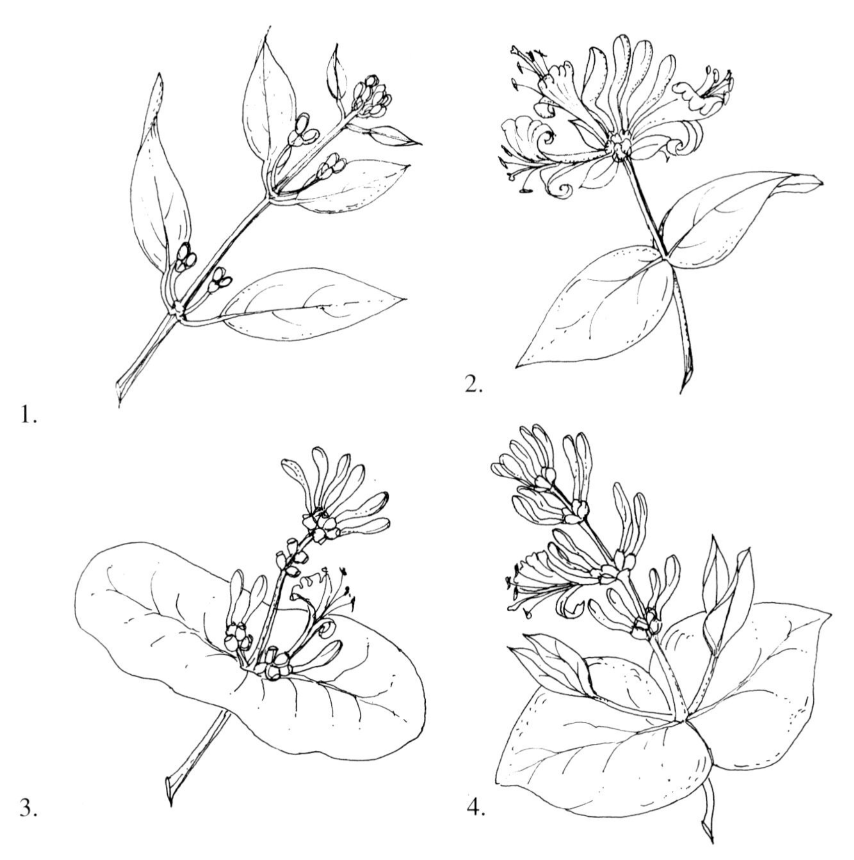

1. *Lonicera alseuosmoides*, showing flowers in pairs, leaves separate, opposite. Group 1a.
2. Orbicular disc of *Lonicera prolifera*. Group 2a.
3. *Lonicera × heckrottii* showing elongated spike and corolla tube divided into two; uppermost with four lobes, lower only one lobe; leaves connate (joined). Group 2b.
4. Dense cluster of *Lonicera periclymenum*. Leaves divided or separate, opposite. Group 2b.

The standard reference on *Lonicera* is Rehder's synopsis of 1903. This still forms the basis for classification today.

The main characteristics are:

Leaves opposite, generally entire, flowers in axillary pairs or in terminal whorls. Corolla tubular, five lobed, generally divided into two. The upper lip with four fused lobes, the lower single lobed. Ovary inferior, the fruit a fleshy berry.

In considering the choice for the garden it is helpful to divide them into two main groups, each group further divided into two.

Lonicera (left) *alseuosmoides*, (right) *giraldii*

Group 1 - Flowers in pairs, leaves separate and evergreen or nearly so.
1a. Unscented, short flowers 3cm or less. Most have interesting foliage and produce colourful berries

Lonicera acuminata Wallich

A narrow-leaved evergreen with ciliate leaves and small cream-yellow, funnel-shaped flowers, often pink blushed. Today, according to botanists, this is a synonym with *L. henryi*, however the two forms in current circulation are horticulturally quite different, *L. henryi* being the better garden plant (see p.9)

Lonicera alseuosmoides Graebn.

A little known Chinese species with striking blue berries in winter. Cream funnel-shaped flowers are purple flushed within during July and August. Narrow, shiny, oblong leaves on non-hairy stems. Suitable for sun or shade, needs protection from cold winds.

Lonicera giraldii Rehd.

The very soft hairy velvety leaves and stems distinguish this from other species. During June and July the terminal clusters of red flowers resemble raspberries, these are then followed by small blue-black berries. Protect from cold winds, suitable for sun or shade but it dislikes winter wet soils.

Lonicera glabrata Wallich

A vigorous Himalayan species with bold green, glossy leaves. The cream and pink

Lonicera (left) *henryi* and (right) *japonica* 'Hall's Prolific' (p.10)

flowers in July and August are followed by very large clusters of shiny black berries. Suitable for sun or shade.

Lonicera henryi Hemsl.
An excellent screening plant for sun or shade with dark green leaves. The orange-pink flowers are produced in June and July and are followed by small blue-black berries in the autumn. A vigorous, hardy and easy plant.

1b. Fragrant, long flowers 4 cm or more. Most are evergreen or nearly so, fragrance is their main feature, berries less significant.

Lonicera japonica 'Aureoreticulata' (T. Moore) Nichols
This is the exception in this group having small fragrant but insignificant flowers. It is grown for its attractive yellow- and green-veined leaves much loved by flower arrangers. The best variegated forms seem most prone to mildew. Part shade in moist ground will help, as will annual cutting back to induce vigorous young stems. Can also be used as ground cover.

Lonicera japonica 'Halliana' (Dipp.) Nichols A.G.M.*
A very widely planted and easily grown honeysuckle. Excellent for rapid screening of sheds, fences and oil tanks in sun or part shade. Because of its powerful fragrance

Lonicera (left) *japonica* var. *repens* and (right) *similis* var. *delavayi* (p.11)

it is also excellent to grow on a pergola near a patio, providing there is room. The white flowers turn yellow after pollination and are produced from July to September. Unfortunately today, plants given this name are very variable. It is therefore better to plant the following form.

Lonicera japonica 'Hall's Prolific' *(see p.9)*

This is supposedly a seedling selection from 'Halliana', introduced and named in Holland in 1985. It is very similar in habit and freedom of flowers to the best forms of 'Halliana'. Better to plant this *selected* form rather than the variable 'Halliana'.

Lonicera japonica 'Horwood Gem'

A sport found in Falmouth and introduced by Peter Adams. It has green- and cream-variegated young leaves which on maturity turn green. The cream flowers are fragrant but smaller than 'Halliana'.

Lonicera japonica var. *repens* Rehd. (*flexuosa* Thunb., *chinensis* Wats.)

This can also be very variable. The best forms have very fragrant purple-crimson and white flowers from July to September and bronze-purple leaves and shoots. It is a vigorous semi-evergreen suitable for sun or part shade and excellent for growing on a pergola. 'Purple Queen' (origin unknown) seems to be identical to the best forms in circulation.

Lonicera japonica 'Acumen' and *japonica* 'Dart's World'

'Acumen' was originally distributed incorrectly under the name of *L. acuminata* but it is quite different. Both of these forms were selected and named by Darthuizer in Holland and are typical *L. japonica* forms, mainly used for ground cover.

Lonicera similis var. *delavayi* (Franch.) Rehd. *(see p.10)*

A very vigorous evergreen, ideal for large pergolas and archways in sun or part shade. The cream and yellow flowers in July and August are larger than 'Halliana' and have longer flower stalks. The flowers therefore are better displayed and stand out against the bold green leaves, making this a very desirable evergreen.

Lonicera hildebrandiana Collett and Hemsl.

This is the giant Burmese honeysuckle and is the largest in flower and leaf of all the honeysuckles. The fragrant cream flowers turn to a rich yellow orange and can be 8 to 12 cm long. Unfortunately it is not hardy except in the very mildest places in Britain. It seldom flowers when young but on maturity, in full sun, will flower freely. Named after a Mr Hildebrand and not spelt with a t!

Group 2 - Flowers in terminal heads or spikes, uppermost leaves joined, many shaped like a disc.

2a. Unscented. Most are brightly coloured and, except the last two, are from North America and Canada

Lonicera (left) *albiflora* (p.12) and (right) *arizonica* (p.12)

Lonicera (left) *hispidula* (p.13) and (right) *prolifera* (p.14)

Lonicera albiflora Torr. and Gray *(see p.11)*

A pleasing semi-evergreen species, slightly bushy in habit with grey-green leaves. The cream and white flowers in June and July are followed by bright orange berries. Sun or part shade.

Lonicera arizonica Rehd. *(see p.11)*

Large terminal clusters of bright orange-red flowers in June and July. The leaves have stipular appendages but the habit is rather sparse. Suitable for sun or part shade but must not get too wet in the winter.

Lonicera × *brownii* (Reg.) Carr

The scarlet trumpet honeysuckle is a hybrid between *L. sempervirens* and *L. hirsuta.* Rehder suggests most forms resemble *sempervirens* more than *hirsuta* and may be the result of recrossing *brownii* with *sempervirens* or reversions. However he goes on to say that despite similarities with *sempervirens* it strongly differs by having a two lipped corolla. The forms of × *brownii* 'Fuchsioides' and × *brownii* 'Punicea' that I have looked at resemble *L. sempervirens* rather than × *brownii*, neither are two-lipped and in neither is the corolla glandular which one would expect.

Lonicera × *brownii* 'Dropmore Scarlet'

A very hardy hybrid of *L. hirsuta* and *L. sempervirens*. It was raised in Canada by Dr Skinner in 1950, the seed parent being *L. hirsuta* as opposed to *L. sempervirens.*

Lonicera (left) *sempervirens* (p.14) and (right) 'Simonet' (p.15)

Deciduous in habit it produces bright orange-red spikes of flowers June until September; the corolla is two-lipped. It is taller than current forms of *L. sempervirens*, flowers more orange but less profuse. Plant in part shade to minimize aphid attack.

Lonicera ciliosa (Pursh) Poir.

A semi-evergreen with blue-green ciliate leaves. The terminal bright yellow-orange flowers form a dense cluster in disc-like leaves, the corolla is very swollen near the base. Flowering in June and very striking in colour but needs protection from mildew.

Lonicera dioica L.

A vigorous deciduous climber with terminal clusters of flowers, pale yellow tinged with pink. The leaves are very glaucous beneath, the ones beneath the flower are fused into large discs. Good clusters of orange-red berries.

Lonicera hirsuta Eaton

Very vigorous deciduous climber. Leaves hairy beneath. The flowers on today's form are bright yellow, in a dense cluster during May and June and these are followed by orange-red berries.

Lonicera hispidula Douglas ex Torr. and A. Gray (*see* p.12)

Deciduous honeysuckle from North America. Grey-green leaves semi-evergreen in southern England. Spikes of flower, cream and purple-pink in July and August. Protect from cold winds.

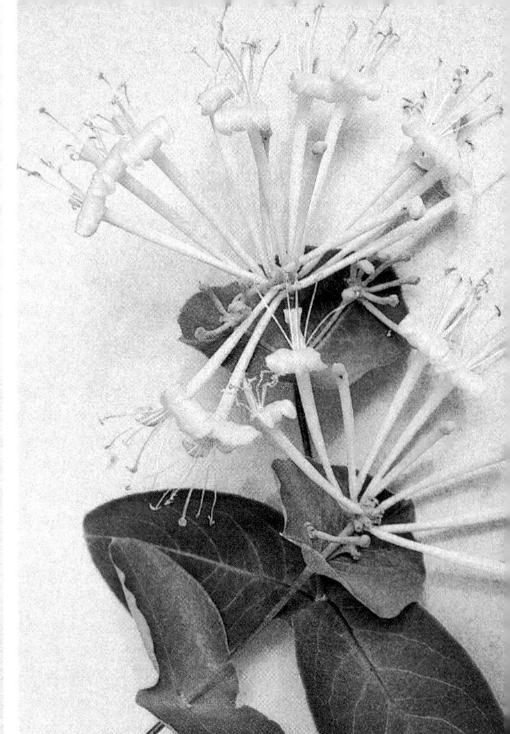

Lonicera (left) × *tellmaniana* (p.15) and (right) *tragophylla* (p.15)

Lonicera pilosa C.D.& R. 1216

This was collected from San Raphael area in Mexico and described as a "very showy climber". It flowered with me for the first time in June 1995 and has pendant whorls of yellow-orange flowers, the corolla being 5 to 6 cm long. The habit is rather sparse (as in *L. arizonica*) but otherwise quite distinct. *Lonicera pilosa* Maxim. is the shrubby *L. strophiophora* so it would seem that this is the *L. pilosa* of Willdenow.

Lonicera prolifera (Kirchn.) Rehd. (*see p.12*)

A lax deciduous twiner with very glaucous stems and leaves. Pale yellow flowers in June on peduncled spikes, usually 2 to 4 whorls. Clusters of yellow and orange berries in the autumn.

Lonicera sempervirens L. A.G.M.* (*see p.13*)

A very long-flowering, semi-evergreen introduced into Britain in the 17th century and grown in John Tradescant's garden. Several forms, including *minor* and *major,* have been introduced but the most common form today gives a profusion of rich orange-scarlet spikes of flower from the end of April until September. Large clusters of orange-red berries are produced from late summer onwards. Protect from cold winds and plant in part shade to reduce the aphid problem. It can look a little untidy after the winter and will benefit from a light prune in the spring to encourage clean new growth.

Lonicera × *americana* (p.16)

Lonicera sempervirens f. *sulphurea* (Jacques) Rehd.

A more vigorous and leggy form with bright yellow flowers produced from the end of June till September. These are followed by yellow berries that later turn red. It can look very effective when grown up through a dark green shrub or conifer. Protect from cold winds.

Lonicera 'Simonet' (*see p.13*)

A Canadian hybrid of uncertain parentage but similar to *L.* × *brownii.* Profuse dense spikes of orange-red flowers in July and August. Deciduous.

Lonicera × *tellmaniana* A.G.M.* (*see p.14*)

A vigorous deciduous hybrid of *L. sempervirens* and *L. tragophylla* raised in Hungary in the 1920s. It has large clusters of copper yellow flowers, tipped with red. It is known in the U.S.A. as 'Redgold'. It makes a bold display in May and June and is valuable for brightening up a shady corner, easier to grow than *L. tragophylla.*

Lonicera × *tellmaniana* 'Joan Sayers'

This plant was selected by Neil Sayers and named after his wife in 1988, from a range of *L.* × *tellmaniana* as the most profuse flowerer with the best colour.

Lonicera tragophylla Hemsl. A.G.M.* (*see p.14*)

A very beautiful Chinese species producing bright golden flowers in June, slightly

Lonicera (left) *caprifolium* 'Anna Fletcher' and (right) *etrusca* 'Donald Waterer' (p.17)

later than *L.* × *tellmaniana*. Not always easy to establish as it needs moisture and shade to grow well, but dramatic when successful. The young leaves are bronze purple tinted, some forms are very purple leaved.

2b. Scented. Mainly of European origin. Leaves below the flower joined, except in the periclymenum forms which include our native woodbine.

Lonicera × *americana* (Mill.) K. Koch (*see also L.* × *italica*)

The true form (p.15) is a beautiful evergreen with pink and cream flowers from July until October. It is a *L. implexa* × *L. etrusca* hybrid and benefits from a sheltered position in sun or part shade.

Lonicera caprifolium L. A.G.M.* (Early Cream)

A vigorous and early flowering honeysuckle, the most common form has cream flushed pink flowers in single whorls subtended by cup-like leaves. It flowers in April and May and is followed by large clusters of orange-red berries. Prune after flowering to encourage clean healthy new growth.

Lonicera caprifolium 'Anna Fletcher'

An excellent form named by Webbs at Droitwich. It has cream- yellow flowers with no trace of pink. Less vigorous than *L. caprifolium*, prune after flowering.

Lonicera (left) 'Goldflame' (p.18) and (right) × *heckrottii* (p.18)

Lonicera caprifolium 'Inga' *(back cover)*

A hairy-leaved form from the Caucasus and originally introduced from Holland as *L. etrusca*. It flowers very early in March and April. Cream flushed pink, smaller than *L. caprifolium* but equally fragrant.

Lonicera caprifolium f. *pauciflora* Carr

All the forms I have looked at, mainly from the West Country, seem to be forms of *L.* × *italica*. They have several whorls of flowers and branch into threes showing the *L. etrusca* influence.

Lonicera etrusca 'Donald Waterer' *(see p.16)*

Found in the French Pyrenees by Donald Waterer, this is more upright in habit than other *L. etrusca* forms and has red stems. The red and cream flowers in July and August are followed by a profusion of orange-red berries. An excellent form which grows happily in full sun and is suitable for container growing.

Lonicera etrusca 'Michael Rosse'

A beautiful form from Nymans Garden, with soft grey-green leaves and cream-yellow flowers. It is less vigorous than 'Superba' (below) and is better planted in sun.

Lonicera (left) × *italica* (p.19) and (right) *periclymenum* 'Belgica' (p.20)

Lonicera etrusca 'Superba' *(front cover)*

A vigorous, sun-loving semi-evergreen with very large trusses of cream and yellow flowers from July to September. A particularly good form came from the Savill Garden at Windsor.

Lonicera 'Goldflame' *(see p.17)*

The name 'Goldflame' is synonymous with *L.* × *heckrottii*, but the form today is different. It is taller, more twining with green rounded deciduous leaves. The flower cluster is shorter and denser, deep pink and yellow-throated. It flowers intermittently from June to September but not in the same profusion as *L.* × *heckrottii.*

Lonicera × *heckrottii* Rehd. *(see p.17)*

A compact, less twining, but floriferous hybrid with very long spikes of pink and orange flowers from June to September. The semi-evergreen, glaucous leaves are narrower and more pointed than 'Goldflame'. Suitable for container growing in part shade.

Lonicera implexa Sol. Minorcan honeysuckle

A sun loving, compact evergreen with cream, yellow and pink flowers from June to August. The single whorls of flowers are subtended by pointed glaucous leaves. Also suitable for container growing.

Lonicera periclymenum (left) 'GrahamThomas' (p.20) and (right) 'Munster' (p.21)

Lonicera implexa 'Lord Ramsay'

This is not *L. implexa* but a *periclymenum* form, not different from other forms.

Lonicera × *italica* Tausch (*see* p.18)

Widely grown as *L.* × *americana*, this is a hybrid of *L. caprifolium* × *L. etrusca*. It is deciduous, very vigorous, free flowering and easy to grow. It generally starts to flower in late April and continues into July. The flowers on the best forms are maroon in bud, pink and yellow on opening. 'Atrosanguinea', *rubella*, 'Cottage Beauty' are some of the forms available and each vary in their depth of colour. Happy growing in sun or part shade.

Lonicera × *italica* 'Harlequin'

Originally described as a sport of 'Belgica' it is in fact an *L.* × *italica* form. Bears typical pink and yellow flowers in May and June and is distinguished by the pink and cream variegated leaves. Less vigorous than type.

Lonicera periclymenum L. Woodbine

Our native honeysuckle grows widely throughout Europe and has given rise to many forms, often very similar to each other.

Lonicera periclymenum (left) 'Serotina' (p.21) and (right) 'Heaven Scent' (p.21)

Lonicera periclymenum 'Belgica'. Early Dutch *(see p.18)*

The widely planted and typical form today has broad green leaves and dense heads of pink and red flowers from early June to the end of July. It produces large clusters of orange-red berries in the autumn. A good garden plant, free flowering, but more vigorous than the original description.

Lonicera periclymenum 'Belgica Select'

In 1977 Boskoop Research Station in Holland released this form, selected as the best of the Belgica forms. In my experience it is too vigorous and not as free flowering as the form described above.

Lonicera periclymenum 'Cream Cloud'

Found near Elspeet in Holland and introduced by H. van der Starre in 1988. Of vigorous habit with large fragrant cream and white flowers similar to 'Graham Thomas'. I have not grown this long enough to compare the two.

Lonicera periclymenum var. *glaucohirta* Kunze

A native honeysuckle from Spain with pointed pubescent leaves and cream and yellow flowers.

Lonicera periclymenum 'Graham Thomas' *(see p.19)*

A vigorous form from a Warwickshire hedgerow. The cream-white flowers turn yellow later and are produced from July to September.

Lonicera periclymenum 'Heaven Scent' *(see p.20)*

A recent selection named by Bill Matthews. Large heads of cream-yellow flowers July and August, very fragrant.

Lonicera periclymenum 'La Gasnerie'

From L. Renault, Orleans, France before 1985. This is described as a beautiful plant similar in colour to 'Belgica' and flowering over a long period June to October. Again I have not had this long enough to make comparisons.

Lonicera periclymenum 'Liden'

Raised in Denmark before 1980. Similar in colour to 'Serotina' but with smaller flowers.

Lonicera periclymenum 'Loly'

From the Plant Breeding Station Lunderskov in Denmark before 1985. Described as very hardy and free flowering. My plant produces white and yellow flowers but not in profusion, certainly not worth growing in southern England.

Lonicera periclymenum 'Munster' (*see p.19*)

A good, easy growing form with pink and cream flowers from June to August. The light green leaves are attractive and do not seem to suffer 'spotting' like some *periclymenum* forms. Origin unknown, possible from Ireland.

Lonicera periclymenum 'Red Gables'

Found at a house in Wick near Pershore. A good free flowering form very similar to *L. periclymenum* 'Serotina' and widely planted. Although some people prefer it to 'Serotina' I have not found it so good.

Lonicera periclymenum var. *reflexa*

Another 'Serotina' form from Hatfield House, origin unknown, name invalid.

Lonicera periclymenum 'Serotina' A.G.M.* Late Dutch (syn. *L.*p. 'Florida') (*see p.20*)

The original 'Serotina' or Late Red of Philip Miller is not what we are growing today. It is probably more like the *semperflorens* of Goldring, i.e. long flowering. Apparently two forms of 'Serotina' have been growing in Holland. The first clone is less vigorous than the second and has been grown in Denmark as 'Florida'. It would appear that this is similar if not identical to the 'Serotina EM85'. This is a very free flowering plant with maroon and cream flowers from July to September. The leaves are narrower and more bronzed than 'Belgica' and is also more compact. The berries also differ in being purple-red.

Lonicera periclymenum 'Serpentine'

This is the second clone of 'Serotina' and was selected from seeds collected by Mr Anton Harkes on the island of Texel (Holland). This is more vigorous than 'Serotina'

Lonicera splendida

with darker leaves and bluish purple-red young stems. In 1988 it was given the cultivar name of 'Serpentine'. The flower is a deeper colour in bud and although it is an attractive plant, it is not so long- or free-flowering as the 'Serotina' of today.

Lonicera periclymenum 'Sweet Sue'

A very free flowering plant from Roy Lancaster with cream and yellow flowers. More compact than 'Graham Thomas'.

Lonicera periclymenum 'Winchester'

Origin unknown, said to grow in U.S.A. and certainly grown in New Zealand. The plant I have is vigorous with strongly twining thin pink red stems. The flowers are similar in size to 'Serotina' but pinker, leaves narrow, grey green. Different, but 'Belgica' and 'Serotina' are better garden plants.

Lonicera splendida Boiss.

A very beautiful evergreen honeysuckle from southern Europe, closely related to *periclymenum.* It has very striking blue grey stems and leaves and dense pink tinged cream flowers. It is not easy to grow and is very subject to mildew. It needs good growing conditions to ripen the wood before the winter and then will produce clusters of orange berries in the autumn.

Footnote:

A.G.M. Award of Garden Merit based on recommendations by Royal Horticultural Society on the plant's value as a good garden plant.

Some honeysuckles for different positions

Sun *L.* × *americana, L. etrusca* - all forms, *L. implexa, L.* × *italica, L. splendida* and most evergreen ones.

Shade *L.* × *brownii* 'Dropmore Scarlet', *L. periclymenum* 'Belgica', 'Munster' and 'Sweet Sue'. *L. sempervirens, L.* ×*tellmaniana, L. tragophylla, L. henryi, L.* ×*heckrottii*

Quick Screening - Evergreen *L. henryi, L. glabrata, L. japonica* cvs, *L. similis delavayii*

Pergolas *L.* × *italica, L. japonica* 'Hall's Prolific', *L. japonica* var. *repens, L. periclymenum* cvs, *L. similis delavayii*

Patio/pots *L.* × *americana, L. etrusca* 'Donald Waterer', *L.* × *heckrottii, L. implexa, L. periclymenum* 'Serotina'

Groundcover *L. japonica* 'Halliana', *L. japonica* 'Acumen', *L. japonica* 'Dart's World', *L. japonica* 'Aureoreticulata', *L. japonica* var. *repens.*

Least susceptible to aphids/mildew
L. etrusca cvs, *L.* × *italica*, all evergreen forms from Group 1 except *L. japonica* 'Aureoreticulata'.

Some honeysuckle combinations

Vigorous honeysuckles with strong twining habit are best grown by themselves but some could be combined with other plants.

L. etrusca 'Donald Waterer' - *Clematis flammula*
L. × *heckrottii* - *Clematis* Jackmanii
L. implexa - *Teucrium fructicans, Clematis* 'Comtesse de Bouchaud'
L. periclymenum 'Serotina' - *Clematis* 'Marie Boisselot' or × *triternata* 'Rubromarginata'
L. sempervirens - through *Pyracantha*

Bibliography

Bean, W.J. 1973 (revised edition) + supplement. *Trees and Shrubs Hardy in the British Isles.* John Murray, London.
Dendroflora, No.25, 1988, pp. 37-54.
Gorer R. and **Harvey J.** *Lonicera* × *americana. The Plantsman,* 1990, Vol 12, pp. 100-104
Hillier Manual of Trees and Shrubs, sixth edition. 1991. Winchester.
Horwood, A.R. *British Wild Flowers,* Vol. III, p. 64. Gresham, London.
Meyer, Paul. Thesis on Genus *Lonicera.* Royal Botanic Garden, Edinburgh
Rehder, A. 1903. *Synopsis of Genus Lonicera.* Missouri Bot. Garden.
Rehder, A. 1990 (2nd Edition). *Manual of Cultivated Trees and Shrubs.* Dioscoroides Press, Portland, Oregon.

My thanks to ALL Kent NCCPG members for supporting this publication.

Index of Plant Names

Figures in bold refer to illustrations.

Lonicera
- acuminata, 8
- albiflora, 12, **11**
- alseuosmoides, 8, **7, 8**
- × americana - *see also* × italica, 16, **15**
- arizonica, 3, 12, **11**
- × brownii, 12
  - Dropmore Scarlet, 5, 12
  - Fuchsioides, 12
  - Punicea, 12
- caprifolium, 5, 16
  - Anna Fletcher, 16, **16**
  - Inga, 17
  - f. pauciflora, 17
- ciliosa, 5, 13
- dioica, 13
- etrusca, 3, 5
  - Donald Waterer, 17, **16**
  - Michael Rosse, 17
  - Superba, 18
- giraldii, 8, **8**
- glabrata, 8
- Goldflame, 18, **17**
- × heckrottii, 4, 18, **7, 17**
- henryi, 9, **9**
- hildebrandiana, 11
- hirsuta, 13
- hispidula, 13, **12**
- implexa, 3, 5, 18
  - Lord Ramsay, 19
- × italica, 4, 5, 19, **18**
  - Atrosanguinea, 19
  - Cottage Beauty, 19
  - Harlequin, 19
  - rubella, 19
- japonica, 4, 5
  - Acumen, 5, 11
  - Aureoreticulata, 5, 9
  - Dart's World, 5, 11
  - Hall's Prolific, 10, **9**
  - Halliana, 9
  - Horwood Gem, 10
  - repens, 10, **10**
- periclymenum, 3, 19, **7**
  - Belgica, 5, 20, **18**
  - Belgica Select, 20
  - Cream Cloud, 20
  - Florida - *see* Serotina
  - glaucohirta, 20
  - Graham Thomas, 4, 20, **19**
  - Heaven Scent, 21, **20**
  - La Gasnerie, 21
  - Liden, 21
  - Loly, 21
  - Munster, 21, **19**
  - Red Gables, 21
  - reflexa, 21
  - semperflorens, 21
  - Serotina, 5, 21, **20**
  - Serpentine, 21
  - Sweet Sue, 22
  - Winchester, 22
- pilosa C.D.& R. 1216, 14
- prolifera, 14, **7, 12**
- sempervirens, 4, 5, 6, 14, **13**
  - f. sulphurea, 5, 15
- similis delavayii, 11, **10**
- Simonet, 15, **13**
- splendida, 5, 22, **22**
- × tellmaniana, 15, **14**
  - Joan Sayers, 15
- tragophylla, 3, 15, **14**